DIANA
A TRIBUTE

DIANA
A TRIBUTE

JULIA DELANO

CRESCENT
BOOKS

Copyright © 1997 Saturn Books.

This edition is published by Crescent Books, a division of
Random House Value Publishing, Inc.,•201 E. 50th Street,
New York, NY 10022, under arrangement with
Ottenheimer Publishers, Inc. BG100A

Crescent Books and colophon are trademarks of
Random House Value Publishing, Inc.

Random House
New York • Toronto • London • Sydney • Auckland
http://www.randomhouse.com/

Printed and bound in Vicenza, Italy.
A CIP catalog record for this book is available from the Library of Congress.

ISBN 0-517-16044-7
8 7 6 5 4 3 2 1

The right of Julia Delano to be identified as the author has been
asserted by the same in accordance with the Copyright, Designs, and
Patents Act 1988.

Cover photo by John Stillwell, 1996, courtesy of "PA" News Photo
Library.

CONTENTS

PAGE 1: *The Princess of Wales at a fundraiser wheelchair race for the International Spinal Research Trust, of which she was a Royal Patron.*

PAGE 2: *Diana in one of the elegant fitted two-piece suits she favoured for daytime engagements.*

LEFT: *Attending the opening day of Ascot in 1987 with her sister-in-law, the Duchess of York.*

Acknowledgments

The publisher would like to thank Mike Rose and Sunita Gahir for designing this book and Nigel Blundell for the final chapter. We would also like to thank the following individuals, institutions and agencies for supplying material:

Bettman Archives: pages 7, 11 (below right), 12 (right), 14, 16 (above), 19 (above), 41, 43 (below), 59, 94.
Bettman/Hulton Collection: page 11 (left).
Hulton Deutsch Collection: pages 6, 8 (right), 9 (both), 10, 62, 63, 64 (bottom), 70 (both), 71

Anwar Hussein: 1, 2, 4, 8 (left), 11 (top right), 12 (left), 13, 15 (both), 16 (below), 17, 18 (both), 19 (below), 20, 21, 22, 23 (both), 24, 25, 26, 27 (both), 28, 29, 30 (all three), 31, 32, 33 (all three), 34 (all three), 35, 36, 37, 38, 39, 40, 42, 43 (above), 45, 46 (bottom), 48, 49, 50, 51, 52 (both), 53, 54 (both), 55, 56 (all three), 57, 58, 64 (top), 69 (top), 78, 79, 80, 81 (all three), 82/3, 84, 85, 86 (both), 87 (both).
Reuters/Bettman Newsphotos: pages 44, 45 (top), 47, 60, 61, 65, 68, 69 (bottom), 72/3, 74 (both), 75, 76 (both), 77.
'PA' News Photo Library: 88, 89, 90, 91, 92, 93, 94 (both), 95, 96 (both).

CHAPTER 1

FROM PONYTAIL TO PRINCESS

ABOVE: *The glamorous Georgiana Spencer (1757-1806), daughter of the first Earl Spencer, married the Duke of Devonshire and also had a much publicised affair with the then Prince of Wales, later George IV.*

RIGHT: *The lonely Princess of Wales: Diana handing out McDonalds Children of Achievement Awards (Spring 1993)*

The announcement on 10 December 1992 that the Prince and Princess of Wales were to separate but not divorce, was received with sorrow but no great surprise, and finally put an end to several years of increasingly intrusive media speculation. There was nothing new in an unhappy royal couple living apart, and the unhappiness of both Diana and Charles in each other's company had been painfully apparent for some time — notably during the disastrous Korean tour which was supposed to reflect a reconciliation. Divorce would follow later, but from the moment of separation Diana vowed to retain her independent life as a full-time career princess and to demonstrate that the role she had created for herself during twelve years of increasingly distant marriage was performed in her own right and not as her husband's wife. It was a vow she would keep right up to her tragic death.

There was little in Lady Diana Spencer's background to suggest that she would develop quite so far between the ages of 20 and 33. She was born on 1 July 1961, the youngest of Earl and Countess Spencer's three daughters. The Spencers really wanted a son and heir to carry on the name and title, and Diana's mother was put under considerable pressure to take medical advice about her tiresome propensity to have daughters. The longed-for son, Charles, now Earl Spencer since his father's death in March 1992, was finally born three years later.

The first-known Spencer was an extremely successful sheep trader in the fifteenth century, and his successors accumulated a substantial fortune, earned an earldom from Charles I and built Althorp House in Northamptonshire. The family remained loyal, dependable and conventional courtiers for three centuries, linked by blood to Charles II and the Dukes of Marlborough, Devonshire, and Abercorn. Technically, in fact, the Spencer family has more royal blood in its lineage than does the House of Windsor.

The marriage of Viscount 'Johnny' Althorp, as he then was, and the Honourable Frances Roche, daughter of Baron Fermoy, was the society wedding of the year in 1954. Frances, at 18, was the youngest girl this century to be married in Westminster Abbey, and the Queen, the Duke of Edinburgh, and Princess Margaret were among

the 1,700 guests. Sadly, what began as a love match ended in an acrimonious and contested divorce when, in 1966, Frances met and fell in love with the flamboyant and extrovert Peter Shand Kydd. Her hopes that she would be allowed to keep the two youngest children, then six and four, were shattered when her own mother, Ruth, Lady Fermoy, testified against her during the hearing of the case.

Diana was brought up in comfortable, indeed privileged, circumstances at Park House in Norfolk, conveniently close to Sandringham, although, contrary to some reports, the family were not on close terms with the royals. After their mother's departure, Diana and her young brother Charles were cared for in Norfolk by a series of nannies while the two older girls, Sarah and Jane, went to a Kent boarding school. All the children continued on a regular basis to see their mother, who initially lived in London, and there was the inevitable rivalry between divorced parents vying for the affection of their young.

Diana's early teenage years produced an unremarkable educational record; her desire to be a ballet dancer was foiled by her height. In 1975 the family left the familiar comfort of Park House for the more forbidding splendour of Althorp when, on the death of his father, Johnny Althorp became the eighth Earl, his son became the Viscount, and his daughters all became Ladies. Further upheaval was caused by his remarriage in 1977 to the former Countess of Dartmouth, daughter of the saccharine romantic novelist Barbara Cartland. The formidable Raine Spencer successfully turned Althorp into a paying proposition in order to meet the crippling debts that the new Earl had inherited, but she was not a wholly welcome addition to the family.

LEFT: *When Diana's parents married in Westminster Abbey in 1954, it was the society wedding of the year.*

ABOVE: *Ruth, Lady Fermoy, Diana's maternal grandmother, deplored the break-up of her daughter's marriage, but was a great support to her royal granddaughter.*

RIGHT ABOVE: *A charmingly informal photograph of Diana Spencer on her first birthday.*

RIGHT BELOW: *The young Diana with her brother Charles, the long-awaited heir and now Earl Spencer.*

LEFT AND BELOW RIGHT: *Diana had a typically comfortable and sheltered aristocratic upbringing.*

TOP RIGHT: *Earl Spencer married Raine, former Countess of Dartmouth in 1976.*

ABOVE LEFT: *The famous photograph of Diana as a nursery teacher.*

School for Diana was followed by the traditional Swiss finishing school, regarded by aristocratic families as the right way to prepare their daughters for the rigours of the social season and the still fairly standard search for a suitable husband. Living a sedate and rather sheltered life in London and weekending at Althorp and a succession of other substantial country seats, Diana did a number of fairly meaningless and menial jobs and babysat for her sister Jane who married Robert Fellowes, now private secretary to the Queen, in 1978. It was sister Sarah who seemed to have the golden prospects, attracting the interest not only of the fabulously rich Duke of Westminster, but even of Prince Charles himself — which is how Lady Diana Spencer came to meet the Prince of Wales in the middle of a field during a day's shooting on the Althorp estate in 1977.

It was a slow process. Diana moved from her mother's Cadogan Square flat to her own establishment in Earl's Court, went skiing, worked as a dance teacher and then moved to the Young England kindergarten school in Pimlico, where she was in her element. In February 1979 she was asked to a Sandringham house party; in July she watched the Prince play polo at Cowdray Park; in August she was invited to join him on the royal yacht *Britannia* for Cowes Week; and in September she went for the first time to Balmoral for the Braemar Games. By then the press were in hot pursuit and had staked out the flat in Coleherne Court. Diana's flatmates acted as decoys, driving her distinctive Metro about London to allow their beleaguered friend some privacy in her romance.

The world's newspapers had already investigated the complete Spencer genealogy, discussed Diana's previous boyfriends (none of them, much to various editors' disappointment, remotely serious), and speculated endlessly about the chances of a royal wedding before the engagement was formally announced on 24 February 1981. The previous six months had been an ordeal by media pack which taught the Princess some invaluable lessons, but the next five, before the wedding on 29 July, were to prove equally stressful.

As soon as the engagement was public, the royal system enveloped this 20-year old kindergarten teacher. Leaving her Earl's Court flat for the last time, Diana was taken by Rolls-Royce to Clarence House, home of the Queen Mother, moving on after a few days to the more large scale life of Buckingham Palace. The sudden and drastic change, and the difficulties Diana faced in coming to terms with the implications of marrying not just a prince, but the heir to the throne, were visibly demonstrated by her dramatic weight loss in the months before the wedding. Her fears that the pressure of royal life would make it difficult to maintain contact with even the closest friends proved well founded. The magnificent ivory silk wedding dress had to be taken in several times in the course of the fitting process.

Everything went off perfectly on the day, of course. The fabulous Glass Coach bore the bride and her father, still shaky from a stroke, safely and promptly to St Paul's Cathedral; the rain held off; the nation took a day's holiday and held its breath in sentimental delight; and Lady Diana Spencer married her prince and became a genuine twentieth-century Fairytale Princess. Perhaps the story should end there, but of course it could not.

LEFT ABOVE: *'It is with the greatest pleasure that the Queen and the Duke of Edinburgh announce the betrothal of their beloved son the Prince of Wales, to Lady Diana Spencer, daughter of the Earl Spencer and the honourable Mrs Shand Kydd.' So went the announcement from Buckingham Palace on 24 February 1981. Prince Charles had proposed and been accepted three weeks before, at a romantic private supper in his apartments at Buckingham Palace.*

RIGHT ABOVE: *A relaxed view of Diana with her fiancé and future mother-in-law, taken at Buckingham Palace.*

RIGHT: *A delightfully casual shot of the engaged couple in robust country clothes, plus a camera-hogging Golden Labrador. Contrary to appearances, however, Diana was not a natural countrywoman, passionate about hunting, shooting and fishing, and this proved an area of stress between husband and wife.*

ABOVE AND LEFT: *The famous strapless black silk taffeta dress, worn by Diana for her first evening engagement as the fiancée of the heir to the throne, earned the disapproval of the Queen Mother. Diana and Princess Grace of Monaco, another commoner who married royalty, found much to say to each other on the same occasion.*

FAR LEFT: *The actual moment of marriage, performed by the Archbishop of Canterbury, Dr Robert Runcie. The text was taken from the 1549 prayer book, although the bride firmly refused to promise to obey. Despite all the rehearsals, both made slight mistakes during the exchange of vows.*

ABOVE: *The wedding of the year, if not the decade, took place on 29 July 1981 in St Paul's Cathedral, rather than the more conventional Westiminster Abbey. The soon-to-be Princess was up at 6.30 am and enjoyed a large breakfast before being delivered into the hands of her hairdresser. She refused to have an elaborate lacquered hairstyle, and there were some who thought that her simple cut was a little too casual and fly-away under the delicate Spencer family tiara. The dress too created problems. Made of English silk and embroidered with tiny pearls and sequins, with wide frilled and scooped neckline and flouncy lace-trimmed sleeves, it was a dream of a wedding dress. The 25-foot long matching train and the veil of ivory tulle gave the bridesmaids a little trouble; here the youngest, Clementine Hambro (great-grand-daughter of Sir Winston Churchill) and Catherine Cameron, follow the bride and groom out of St Paul's.*

LEFT: *Escorted by her father, a veiled Lady Diana Spencer enters the cathedral for the nerve-wracking 3½ minute walk to the altar, to the sound of massed trumpets playing Jeremiah Clarke's Trumpet Voluntary.*

RIGHT: *Leaving the Cathedral, the new Princess has thrown back her veil, dotted with ten thousand tiny hand-embroidered mother-of-pearl sequins, to reveal a cool, exquisite face. Her cascading bouquet consists of yellow roses, freesias, lily-of-the-valley and a sprig of myrtle for luck.*

ABOVE: *A thousand doves fluttered up into the blue sky as the newlyweds travelled in their open carriage from St Paul's back down Fleet Street and the Strand to Buckingham Palace.*

LEFT: *Urged on by the hugely enthusiastic crowd, Prince Charles first gracefully kissed his wife's hand and then — when that was not enough — her lips, the first ever public kiss on that balcony.*

ABOVE RIGHT: *The formal wedding photograph, taken at Buckingham Palace after the ceremony, shows the bride and groom surrounded by both families and a charming group of pages and bridesmaids.*

BELOW RIGHT: *The obligatory greeting from the palace balcony.*

CHAPTER 2

DIANA AS STYLE LEADER

RIGHT: *The Princess wears her mother-in-law's wedding gift to her, in turn inherited from Queen Mary: a diamond tiara with pendant pearls and a central lover's knot in French eighteenth-century style, which is saved for what the royals term a 'big dressing day'. Here it is matched with diamond and sapphire drop earrings.*

RIGHT: *A slimline and flattering fitted jacket in turquoise, a favourite colour, makes a practical outfit for a long day of public engagements and walkabouts. Diana invariably acquired an armful of posies whenever she met the public.*

No one who saw the engagement photographs of Lady Diana Spencer, looking slightly plump in her unflattering blue suit bought off-the-peg from Harrods and peering shyly up from under her long hair, could have predicted that well within ten years she would be an international fashion leader and hailed as one of the world's best-dressed and most elegant women. The poise that came with knowing that she was doing a difficult and demanding job well, and had the ability to charm almost any audience, gave Diana a much-needed sense of self-worth and an assurance that further enhanced her natural good looks. In fact, at one stage in the long drawn out speculation about the royal break-up, a number of American fashion houses happily considered the possibility of offering the ex-Princess of Wales a top modelling job. She herself, however, said that clothes were not her priority and cultivated a more serious image with her work as a charity patron; she wanted to achieve something more tangible than simply looking good, which at one stage seemed to be all that was expected of her.

Just the same, her wardrobe was epic by any standard and she is sometimes credited with reviving single-handed the flagging British fashion industry. A recent survey suggested that in the decade after her marriage she spent close on £1 million ($1½ million) on clothes, and that does not take account of her private clothes.

Clothes for her official engagements were planned weeks in advance and only a radical change of weather would prompt a change of plan. It took two full-time

LEFT: *To meet the Vienna Boys Choir in April 1985, Diana wears a white coat dress with a deep black ruffle edging one side of the neckline, designed by Catherine Walter.*

ABOVE LEFT: *With Prince William at Aberdeen Airport on the way to Balmoral, wearing an elegant tailored coat with classic velvet collar.*

ABOVE RIGHT: *This ornate cream suit, with its tight skirt and jagged hemline, here seen as the royals wait at Victoria Station to greet the Spanish royal family, provoked fashion disapproval.*

dressers to organize the royal wardrobe, and to keep a detailed record of what had been worn on each occasion. The size and sumptuousness of this collection of clothes did provoke critical comment: but then so did the occasions when she wore an already familiar outfit once too often. Prince Charles was once asked teasingly by a cheeky photographer, 'Why can't you buy your wife a new frock then?' In later years designers like Versace would provide her with wonderful clothes but she would eventually auction many of her most glamorous outfits for charity, on the suggestion of her son William.

The natural style of the nineteen-year old Diana Spencer was that of any well-born young woman about town: striped shirts, Benetton sweaters, flat shoes and hooped earrings. The house of Hartnell, who traditionally design elaborate, formal evening dresses for the senior royal ladies, held no attractions for her. Instead her sister Jane, who had worked at *Vogue* magazine as an editori-

al assistant before her marriage, introduced the Princess-to-be to the then *Vogue* fashion team: fashion editor Anna Harvey, beauty editor Felicity Clark and former model Grace Coddington. They summoned clothes from designers' showrooms all over London for Diana to try, and encouraged her to develop her natural taste. The first sign that she was beginning to develop the confidence to establish her own style was the stunningly low-cut strapless black dress she wore to a formal dinner at the Goldsmiths' Hall, London, shortly before her wedding.

David and Elizabeth Emmanuel, who designed both the daring Goldsmiths' dress and the gloriously romantic ivory silk wedding dress, split up and vanished from the scene, but some of the top designers selected by the Princess in those early days remained mainstays of the royal wardrobe. These included Jasper Conran, whose elegant wool suits were perfect for Diana's daytime needs, while his fun evening wear was ideal for less

formal occasions. Catherine Walker of the Chelsea Design Company was another regular, and Rifat Ozbek and Victor Edelstein both supplied glamorous evening gowns.

The Princess's favourite colours were rich, warm shades of red, purple, pink and turquoise that set off her blonde hair and tanned skin so well. She rarely wore man-made fabrics; in winter she wore wool jersey or wool crêpe, which do not crease too badly, and in summer she preferred silk crêpe to either linen or cotton. She mastered all the secrets of the fashion trade; smoothing her skirt from the back and always wearing a silky petticoat to match her outfit. Skirts could not be too short or, as she said, 'When I bend over there are six children

looking up it.' Hems were weighted to avoid any possibility of the wind revealing more of the royal legs than was seemly, and sleeves could also be a problem.

Diana's private wardrobe was a different matter altogether; when she went out with friends she saw no reason why she should not dress to please herself. The results were, to say the least, eye-catching — fake ostrich skin jodhpurs, for example, or brightly-coloured silk waistcoats from a men's outfitters. Sometimes her fun outfits had the fashion pundits sorrowfully shaking their heads, although they were usually gladly copied by the royal-watching public. The combination of black satin bomber jacket, ruffled blouse, red leather trousers and high heels,

Her make-up was simple and understated, concentrating on gold blusher (which also helped to disguise her tendency to flush when hot or stressed) and pink lipstick. Her main trademark was the line of sapphire blue eyeliner along the lower rim of her eyes, a tip picked up from ever-glamorous film star Elizabeth Taylor.

Jewellery is an essential feature of any royal lady's wardrobe, and Diana was instrumental in making the wearing of extravagant, sometimes jokey, jewels trendy among the younger set with whom she mixed. The delicate tiara she wore for her wedding was a Spencer treasure; other wedding presents included Queen Mary's tiara in a lover's knot design of diamonds and pearls. Another Queen Mary jewel was a cabochon emerald and diamond Art Deco necklace which the Princess sported as a headband on one royal tour, when her neck was too sunburned to allow wearing it as a choker. Foreign tours often involved the giving of fabulous jewels, and some of Diana's most elaborate jewellery came from the Crown Prince of Saudi Arabia, who presented her with a stunning sapphire suite which included not one but two necklaces, one a sunburst pendant and one a choker. For less dressy occasions, Butler and Wilson in London's Fulham Road supplied the fashion-conscious Princess with many a sparkling piece of diamanté.

which she wore for her third visit to Andrew Lloyd Webber's staggeringly successful musical *Phantom of the Opera,* was generally agreed to be a disaster. Even on formal engagements there was an occasional miscalculation, like the ornate cream suit with heavy gold braiding, tight shirt and v-shaped hemline the Princess wore to the passing-out parade at Sandhurst Military Academy one year. And, of course, a single mistake caused far more comment than any number of classic, elegant outfits.

After the unhappiness of her private life and her well publicised eating disorders, in later years Diana came to terms with herself and her body, discovering the pleasure of a fitness regime. Swimming, workouts and a controlled diet took care of her figure even after two pregnancies.

LEFT: *This memorable ensemble of polka dots, worn to a polo match in 1986, started a fashion trend.*

ABOVE: *Cool in flowing pale green silk and matching shady hat for a visit to Nigeria.*

RIGHT: *The Prince and Princess of Wales in nineteenth-century dress during a visit to the Klondike in 1983.*

LEFT: *Sometimes Diana's private style influenced her more formal wardrobe, as in this elegant matador-style trouser suit.*

ABOVE: *This black hat with its long face-net had an appropriate air of solemnity for the Remembrance Day service.*

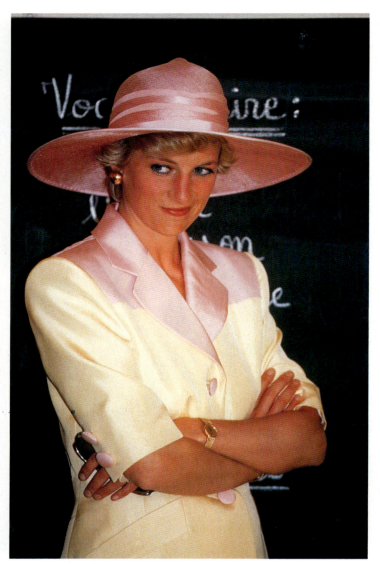

ABOVE: *For royalty hats are never out of fashion, but Diana's individual and stylish wearing of them brought them back into vogue as a fashion accessory. This wonderfully zingy ensemble graced a number of formal occasions.*

ABOVE: *A simple deep-crowned style. There were approximately 75 hats in the royal wardrobe, all kept meticulously stored in tissue paper and dust-free hat boxes. Initially the Scottish-born milliner John Boyd supplied most of the Princess's hats; later she patronized Graham Smith and Philip Somerville, who created many of her larger and more sophisticated hats.*

RIGHT: *In Dubai in 1989 Diana chose her favourite skullcap-style overlaid with a wide flat white brim tilted rakishly over one eye with suit to match.*

RIGHT: *Another delightfully cool confection in turquoise and white.*

ABOVE: *In Melbourne in 1988 the Princess wore a strapless pink and blue evening dress by Catherine Walker; it was split up one side and had a large bow flaring from the hip. Her pinned-back hair emphasized the magnificent diamond and sapphire jewels.*

ABOVE: *Black velvet and red taffeta combined in a dramatic flamenco-style gown with graduated hem and layers of black net underskirts; note the contrasting gloves, a daring and jokey touch!*

LEFT: *Diana in a heavy white satin dress with matching bolero jacket arrives at New York's 'Wintergarden' for a formal dinner in February 1989.*

LEFT: *A long knotted rope of pearls shows off the Princess's elegant back in a plunging crushed velvet dress, worn for the premiere of the film* Back to the Future.

ABOVE: *Diana in a chic black evening dress during dinner in Versailles in 1994*

ABOVE: *A smiling Princess of Wales wearing an elegant suit during the wedding of Viscount Linley to Serena Stanhope*

RIGHT: *A modern princess in every aspect—Diana in a very modest but charming black dress so different from the ones she used to wear decorated with ruffles and frills.*

RIGHT: *The slicked-back hairstyle that the Princess of Wales wore during her stay in New York in January 1995 caused such a sensation that it was described by newspapers all over the world.*

DEVOTED MOTHER

ABOVE: *The doting parents leave the hospital with*
Prince William.

RIGHT: *Princesses too find pregnancy tiring; this blue cotton*
maternity dress by Catherine Walker, worn here at a polo
match at Windsor in May 1982, was one of Diana's favourites.

In conversation with veteran television personality Alastair Burnet in 1985, the Princess of Wales modestly described her role as 'supporting my husband whenever I can, and always being behind him, encouraging him. And also, most important, being a mother and a wife.' While it was painfully clear well before the separation that Diana no longer felt able to support her husband, there is no dispute whatever about the close and loving relationship between her and her two sons.

Within three months of marriage, Diana was pregnant. Like many women, she felt worst in the first few months, before her condition was obvious or a formal announcement had been made. A three-day tour of Wales in October 1981 was made miserable by morning sickness, and it was a relief when official confirmation of the pregnancy, on 5 November 1981, enabled her to discuss her condition with wellwishers. Prince William Arthur Philip Louis was born at 9.00 pm on 21 June 1982, in the private Lindo wing of St Mary's Hospital, Paddington, under the benign supervision of veteran royal gynaecologist George Pinker, and with Prince Charles in anxious attendance. Within two years the Princess was pregnant again;

this time the announcement was made, rather touchingly, on Valentine's Day, 14 February 1984. Henry Charles Albert David followed his brother into the world at 4.20pm on 15 September, after a faster and easier labour. The boys' first names were Diana's choice, with Charles's preference for Arthur amd Albert relegated to middle names.

Within the constraints of security and the royal schedule, Diana tried to ensure that her sons lived as normal a life as possible. In their early days they were cared for by the redoutable Barbara Barnes, an informal, independent-minded, and extremely experienced nanny who developed a good relationship not only with the boys but also with their mother.

It was Diana's suggestion that both William and Harry should attend nursery school, rather than the more usual royal pattern of employing a governess to educate them in the privacy of Kensington Palace in the early years. The choice of a school only a mile away, in Notting Hill, enabled the boys both to lead an almost normal school life and to see as much as possible of their parents. From there each moved on at the age of seven to Wetherby, a

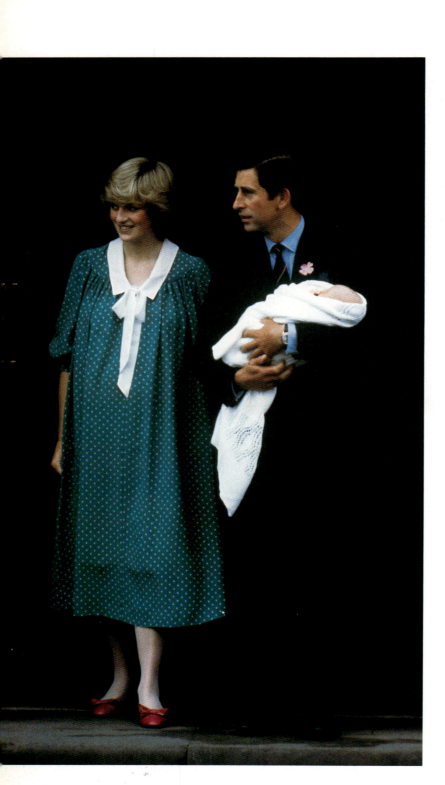

ABOVE: *Prince Charles stayed with his wife throughout her difficult sixteen-hour labour and conducted her back to Kensington Palace less than a day later, when she firmly decided she was ready to come home.*

RIGHT: *Prince William was christened in a small family ceremony in the music room in Buckingham Palace on the Queen Mother's eighty-second birthday. He let out three small protesting squawks when sprinkled with Jordan water by the Archbishop of Canterbury, but was soon soothed by a maternal finger.*

select and expensive pre-prep day school. In autumn 1990 William moved on again, this time as a boarder, to Ludgrove preparatory school in Berkshire, to be followed by his brother two years later, leaving the Princess with a empty nest in Kensington Palace, at least in term time.

The two family homes were Kensington Palace and Highgrove in Gloucestershire. Following the separation the Kensington apartments continued to be occupied by Diana and the boys when they were with her, while Charles remained at Highgrove with an apartment in Clarence House. Diana was influential in the redecoration carried out at Kensington Palace, and ensured that the bedrooms, nursery suite and two studies were kept cheerful, light and airy as befitted a family home; the formal reception rooms have a much more majestic and sombre tone.

The two princes were not the only junior residents of Kensington Palace. Their royal neighbours included Prince and Princess Michael of Kent and their two children, Lord Frederick and Lady Gabriella Windsor, and the Duke and Duchess of Gloucester and their three children, the Earl of Ulster, Lady Davina, and Lady Rose Windsor. Diana's sister Lady Jane Fellowes and her husband, the Queen's private secretary Sir Robert Fellowes, lived in a grace-and-favour house nearby and their two daughters, Laura and Alexandra, were yet more company for their two princely cousins. There were so many royal children that, when they were all younger, Diana considered setting up a kindergarten within the palace, and their cheerful presence added immeasurably to its life and vibrancy.

The young princes also had their own private walled garden, well stocked with swings and climbing frames for the agile boys. Many an informal photographic session was held here, but the Princess tried to protect her children from too much exposure to the media, telling them firmly that the photographers were more interested in her. Despite her attempts to prevent William, in particular, from being spoilt by the inevitable attention, he showed when younger the occasional flash of royal arrogance. When he earned himself a cuff on the head from his mother at a school sports day in 1990, childcare experts were disapproving but other parents sympathised. There was also an alarming occasion when Prince William shot out of the door of the Waleses' apartment, straight into the path of a reversing Jaguar, to be plucked out of harm's way at the very last moment by his furious and frightened mother.

When in London Diana tried to spend as much time with her sons as possible, despite her full working diary. In the days when both boys were at day school she would often reschedule her appointments so that she could pick them up from school and then take them straight to Buckingham Palace for a swim in the royal pool. She also liked personally to do as much of the clothes shopping for them as she could, and was frequently seen buying

LEFT: *After Harry's birth Diana again left hospital within 24 hours, this time looking much more glamorous, in a red dress and with her hair blonder.*

ABOVE: *For Harry's christening the Princess, who was herself godmother to over 20 children, was able to choose more personal friends as godparents, including ex-flatmate Carolyn Pride and artist Brian Organ.*

matching shorts and sweaters in the junior Benetton in Kensington (she said that otherwise there were arguments).

The pace of life was more relaxed at Highgrove, and the Princess was able to enjoy the company of her children in a more homelike setting, but she is reported never to have felt fully at home there and escaped back to London whenever she could. The two princes were promising horsemen, in the royal tradition, but their mother was less enthusiastic about the sport. Highgrove is a delightful eighteenth-century Georgian country house in a characteristically English style which is not dissimilar to Park House where Diana spent her childhood. It

has a rambling garden with wildflower walks and fruit trees, an old-fashioned kitchen garden, and an organic farm — of particular interest to Prince Charles. A rosemary hedge masks the swimming pool where the Princess used to take her daily dip.

Perhaps because they lived in such close proximity to other members of the royal family in London, the Waleses rarely invited any of them to Highgrove, although Princess Anne's country home was only a few miles away. Diana never enjoyed particularly close relationships with her royal in-laws, but she grew closer to her own mother, Frances Shand Kydd, at this time and holidayed more than once in the Caribbean with her and the boys.

LEFT: *Some commentators were shocked when Diana insisted on taking the six-month old Prince William on an extended tour of Australia and New Zealand in spring 1983, but she was determined not to be separated from her son for any length of time. Here the family poses for an informal photo call in New Zealand*

ABOVE: *Prince William and his parents pose for photographers in the gardens of Kensington Palace: the one-year old prince is well wrapped up against the autumn cold.*

RIGHT: *In the family apartment in Kensington Palace.*

ABOVE: *A charmingly relaxed family snapshot on holiday in Majorca in 1987.*

RIGHT: *Prince William's second birthday was recorded with a photo session in the private garden at Kensington Palace; the Princess was six months pregnant at the time.*

LEFT: *Visiting the Niagara Falls, Canada, in 1991, mother and sons are well protected against the spray.*

BELOW: *A thoroughly English tradition: the Mother's Race at Sports Day. On the first occasion the competitive Princess won, but she only came third this time.*

RIGHT: *The Princess of Wales with her sons greeting people gathered after a Mass in Sandringham, Norfolk, on Christmas Day 1994. This kind of unofficial meeting helped Diana prepare William and Harry for monarchical duties that they will have to fulfill in the future.*

DIANA AT PLAY

ABOVE AND RIGHT: *Ascot was a favourite social occasion and always found the Princess looking her best and most relaxed. Here she is seen with the Duchess of York, another royal bride whose marriage went sour.*

The Princess of Wales developed immeasurably in poise and self-assurance over the years — in the early days the rigours of a public engagement could reduce her to private tears, and this was reflected very clearly in her determination to choose her own leisure activities. Constantly on display and playing a role in her working life, Diana recognized the need to find time to relax and be herself, and carefully built this into her working day.

Her routine would begin with a quick dash to Buckingham Palace for twenty or thirty brisk lengths, breaststroke, in the heated indoor pool. She would return with her hair still wet for a session with her regular hairdresser. Sometimes these early morning runs were extended to include the fulfilment of a personal ambition, such as visiting the BBC's television news studios or sitting in silently on the early morning show on Capital Radio, her favourite radio channel.

On an off-duty day in London, Diana's usual pattern was to spend the morning on royal business, first discussing future engagements with her equerry and lady-in-waiting, then perhaps meeting officials from one

of the charities she was involved with or studying sketches and samples for the royal wardrobe with one of her couturiers. She may have slipped out in jeans and a headscarf to do her own shopping, perhaps wheeling her own trolley round Safeway or visiting a local bookshop for the light novels she enjoyed, though a discreet bodyguard would always be close by. She also went regularly on more formal shopping trips, to Covent Garden and Bond Street as well as the smart Chelsea and Kensington stores favoured by rich young women.

If she were having lunch at home, she might well have invited a girlfriend to join her — one of a select group of true confidantes with whom she could enjoy a proper gossip. These included her former flatmates, Carolyn Bartholomew and Virginia Pitman, who had remained close friends of the Princess since the pre-engagement days when they had loyally helped her dodge unwelcome media attention. Traditionally royalty have looked to the aristocracy for their immediate social circle, and Diana was no exception. Other close and trusted friends were Milly Soames, daughter of the Lord Lieutenant of Herefordshire, and her brother, banker Philip Dunne,

James Gilbey, Kate Menzies of the publishing clan, Catherine Soames, and Lady Romsey. The Duchess of York was a regular visitor while she was still plain Sarah Ferguson and during the early days of her marriage, but the relationship cooled before the Yorks' separation was announced. Lunch was light, often vegetarian, with salads a must. Alternatively the Princess may have met friends at one of a number of favourite restaurants, perhaps Launceston Place in Kensington, Luigi's in Covent Garden or Green's in Mayfair, with the occasional foray to the Chinese restaurant Mr Wings for a change from traditional European cooking.

Other forms of relaxation included the occasional trip to the local Odeon cinema in Kensington High Street or a comfortable night in front of the television. Favourite shows included Australian soap *Neighbours*, *Brookside*, chat shows — and the satirical show *Spitting Image*, which mercilessly lampooned the royal family among its many other victims. In the early days of her marriage the Princess earned the reputation of listening to nothing but pop music on her Walkman, but in fact her tastes were catholic, and she may equally well have listed to one of the great romantic composers such as Grieg, Schumann or Rachmaninov. In her circle every well-brought up girl learned piano throughout her school career.

Fitness became almost an obsession with Diana, particularly after her acknowledged eating disorders; her dramatic weight loss both before her marriage and after William's birth was due as much to a rigorous exercise programme as to stress or dieting. Stress and fatigue were an inevitable part of the balancing act of being royal, however, and Diana combated them by keeping her body toned and supple. As well as regular swimming, she worked out to a keep-fit video and did a regular dance routine, which she described as a mix of jazz, tap and ballet. There were some eyebrows lifted among the more traditional members of the royal circle when the Princess of Wales appeared on stage at Covent Garden in a rou-

LEFT AND ABOVE: *Since Prince Charles is a keen polo player, Diana inevitably found herself, particularly in the early days of her marriage before she began to develop her own interests, spending some of her leisure hours watching polo matches. Here she rewards the winners; one of them with a kiss.*

tine choreographed specially for her by ballet dancer Wayne Sleep, but no one could deny the quality of the performance.

Another form of exercise favoured by the sporty Princess was tennis, and she was a member of the exclusive Vanderbilt Club in Shepherd's Bush, West London. Some discreet coaching greatly improved her game, and she enjoyed a much-publicised match with champion Steffi Graf, as well as more evenly matched battles with Julia Dodd-Noble, nicknamed 'Crown Jewels' because she knew so many royals.

Holidays were always a more delicate issue in the Waleses' household. Although the Princess was photographed at Balmoral during her honeymoon looking idyllically happy in her heathery Scottish surroundings, she was not enamoured of the hearty country routine of shooting and fishing that the royal family adopted on holiday. The Queen usually stays at Balmoral from early August, immediately after Cowes Week, until well into October, and other members of the royal family are expected to join her. Much more to Diana's taste was the week she and the boys spent each year with King Juan Carlos and Queen Sofia of Spain and their family in one of their summer homes.

The favourite was the Marivent Palace in Majorca, overlooking the Palma Yacht Club, combined with leisurely sea cruises on the sumptuous Spanish royal yacht. Another holiday destination that was more to the

TOP: *A visit to Balmoral was supposed to be a holiday, but there were inevitable social duties, such as the Braemar Games, which Diana enjoyed less than some of her in-laws.*

ABOVE: *Scottish weather is notoriously unreliable.*

RIGHT: *Arriving at Aberdeen Airport on the way to Balmoral.*

ABOVE: *With Prince Charles at Klosters; although cooperative on this occasion, Diana's relationship with the press was often angry and ultimately tragic.*

RIGHT: *The Princess with the Duke and Duchess of York, all well muffled up against the biting cold.*

FAR RIGHT: *Returning exhausted after a long day on the ski slopes, the Princess would be fully recovered in a few hours and ready for some nightlife.*

Princess's taste was Princess Margaret's Caribbean hide-away on the beautiful and secluded island of Mustique.

One holiday taste that the Princess did share with her husband was skiing. Together with a group of friends, they made annual visits to Klosters in the Swiss Alps, until the tragic accident in 1988 when Major Hugh Lindsay, former equerry to the Queen and a good friend of both the Prince and Princess of Wales, was killed by an avalanche.

The Princess had learned to ski as a teenager and, while not a daredevil skier like her husband or the Duchess of York, enjoyed both the sport and *après-ski* social life that was an integral part of it. Although Prince Charles went back to Klosters after the 1988 accident, the Princess stayed away. Another skiing holiday, in March 1992 at Lech in Austria, also ended unhappily, interrupted by the news of her father's death.

ABOVE, RIGHT AND FAR RIGHT: *Holidays with the Spanish royal family at the Marivent Palace on Majorca had become a regular feature of the summer and were far more to Diana's taste than the hearty outdoor life of Balmoral. Diana and the boys enjoyed the beach and pool, while Charles was more inclined to drive up into the hills for some sketching.*

ABOVE: *In a carefree mood at Marivent Palace, though the sunshine seems to be getting to Harry. Prince Charles and Queen Sofia of Spain are in the background.*

RIGHT: *Trim and lovely in a bikini after two pregnancies.*

OVERLEAF: *A relaxed and happy Princess of Wales chatting with guests at a dinner held in Versailles Palace in 1994.*

CHAPTER 5

CARING PRINCESS: CHARITY AND ARTS WORK

ABOVE: *In her role as patron of the charity Help the Aged, Diana visited Bridges community project in Gwent in 1987.*

RIGHT: *The prize-giving and graduation ceremony of the Royal Academy of Music, held at St Marylebone's Church, 1985.*

As the attraction of dressing up and simply being admired began to pall, Diana became a career princess, increasingly aware of her high-profile value as a fund-raiser and charity patron. This was not, however, a totally new departure for her; the boarding school she attended in her early teens, West Heath in Kent, encouraged its pupils to become involved in the local community. Diana and a friend regularly visited an old lady in Sevenoaks, doing some housework and shopping for her, and she also worked for the local Voluntary Service Unit, visiting mentally and physically handicapped patients at a local hospital.

Initially Diana's work as patron was mainly in the arts field; she counted RADA (the Royal Academy of Dramatic Arts), the Royal Academy of Music and the English National Ballet among the imposing bodies of which she was president. Rather more surprising was her role as Colonel-in-Chief of a number of regiments. After the assassination of Lord Mountbatten, she was invited to succeed him as Colonel-in-Chief of the Royal Hampshires, the last royal line regiment affiliated to a single county. She was also Colonel-in-Chief of the 13/18th Royal Hussars and the Princess of Wales' Own Regiment of Canada, and Honorary Commandant, RAF Wittering, which entailed reading massive folders of papers on defence issues.

A more personal sense of involvement was reflected in the work the Princess did for family-related charities. One of her earliest commitments in this field was to Dr Barnardo's children's homes, of

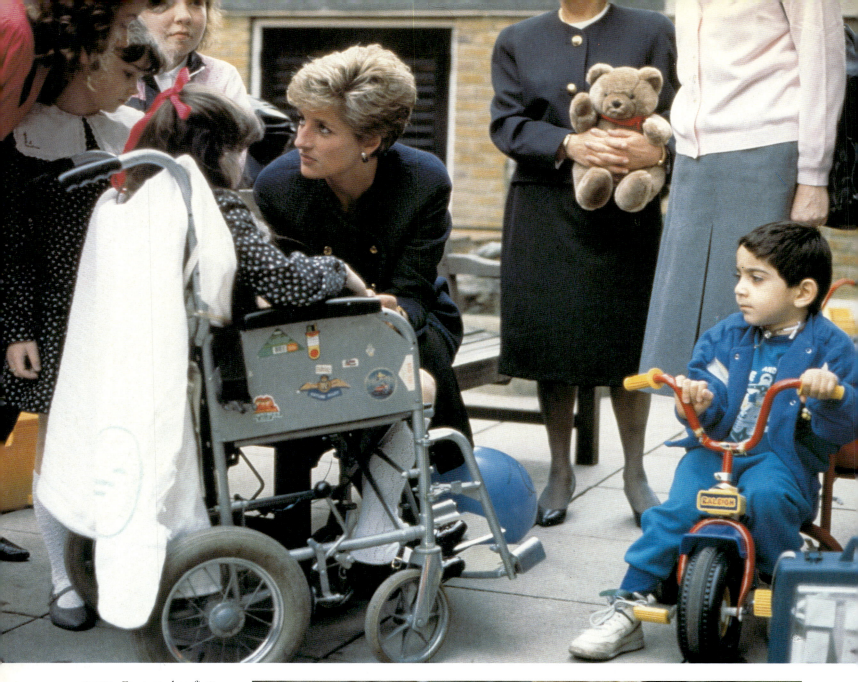

ABOVE: *Even on her first official tour to Wales in 1981, Diana proved that she had a natural way with children. Ten years later the passionate concern was undiminished as the Princess visited Great Ormond Street Hospital for Children in March 1991.*

RIGHT: *A Barnardo day care centre in Brixton, South London.*

FAR RIGHT: *Young Sara, aged five, presented the Princess with flowers and was lifted on to the royal lap during a visit to a home for abused children in Kingston, Canada, in October 1991.*

which she was an extremely active president for many years. She had the natural gift of accepting people at face value and putting them at their ease. When Barnardo's asked her to sign a 'Children's Charter', she arranged for three mentally handicapped children to join the ceremony in the Waleses' Kensington Palace apartment, and responded cheerfully to an off-the-cuff request for a guided tour. While her role as president gave a wonderful boost to fund-raising, it was individual visits that gave most pleasure, and the Princess was as generous with her time as with her purse.

She made a point of keeping abreast of family-related issues that hit the headlines. One such issue was that of child abuse, sparked by the controversial diagnosis of multiple abuse in a large number of families in Cleveland, northern England. As a result Diana became involved with Childline, a charity established by television personality Esther Rantzen to offer abused children a confidential telephone help and advice service. On a number of visits the Princess sat and listened as volunteers manned the phones and she heard some horrifying tales. As well as making substantial donations herself, her involvement and interest helped to raise the charity's profile and increased the flow of funds.

Her most significant role was the support she gave to less obviously popular charities. When she visited a purpose-built ward for AIDS sufferers in April 1987, at a time when there was a considerable public hysteria about the disease, her gesture achieved more than any government education programme. She met nine terminally ill men, shook their hands, sat on their beds and talked to them about their condition in a way that medical staff, not normally noted for their susceptibility, found 'very moving'.

Diana's close involvement in AIDS fund-raising and counselling required considerable personal bravery in facing the social taboos surrounding a disease with no cure. The death in 1991 from AIDS of a close friend, Adrian Ward-Jackson, well known for his work in the arts world, reinforced this commitment. She took on the role of patron of the National AIDS Trust, making her first appearance in that capacity in April 1991 with a speech she wrote herself: 'HIV does not make people dangerous to know, so you can shake hands and give them a hug — heaven knows they need it.' Some months earlier she had flown to Washington DC on a one-day fund-raising trip and made a point of visiting a home for children with AIDS, an experience that left more than one of her staff close to tears.

The Princess's growing interest in and commitment to the charities with which she worked extended into the wider implications of the social issues that they raised. She tried to focus on this in

speeches on family life, drug and alcohol abuse and the problems of old age, but was still a nervous and hesitant speechmaker. Film director Sir Richard Attenborough was an encouraging coach, teaching her to take a slow breath at the end of each sentence so that she did not speak too fast and telling her when to smile or raise her head, so that the speech flowed in a natural rhythm.

Another cause that was close to her heart was drug abuse, and she hosted a reception at Kensington Palace for Turning Point, a charity which concerns itself with both drug and alcohol abuse. Interestingly she was more hesitant about becoming involved with the marriage guidance counselling service Relate, turning down the first approach to become its patron. Since becoming Princess of Wales she had been approached for support by well over two hundred organisations and took care to be selective. The negative response to Relate was accompanied by an offer to visit their headquarters in Rugby to learn more about their operation. She was sufficiently impressed to become actively involved in counselling sessions.

When Relate approached her again she was happy to agree, and subsequently attended private role-play sessions for trainee counsellors, where her sympathetic interaction prompted Relate's director to describe her as 'perceptive and intuitive . . . she would make a very good addition to our team because she is such a natural communicator.'

The image of the do-gooding aristocrat was both attractive and contentious, and swiftly became as clichéed as the phrase 'Caring Princess'. When *Vanity Fair* described her as a saint, other journalists sharpened their knives, and the Princess herself was mortally embarrassed; being put on a pedestal or hailed as an angel of mercy because of short visits and natural charm in her view devalued the work of those many workers who devoted themselves full-time to the causes she supported. But she also knew, as one AIDS patient told her, that 'One handshake from you is worth a million words from us.'

ABOVE: *At an earlier visit to Great Ormond Street Hospital for Children, Diana still sported the longer hairstyle she had worn for her wedding.*

RIGHT: *Undaunted by the weather on a visit to a project being carried out by Oldham and Rochdale Groundwork Trust at Princess Park, Oldham.*

RIGHT: *The Princess got closely involved at the International Deaf Youth Rally in South Glamorgan. When asked to address an international convention for the deaf, she delighted her audience by 'signing' her speech.*

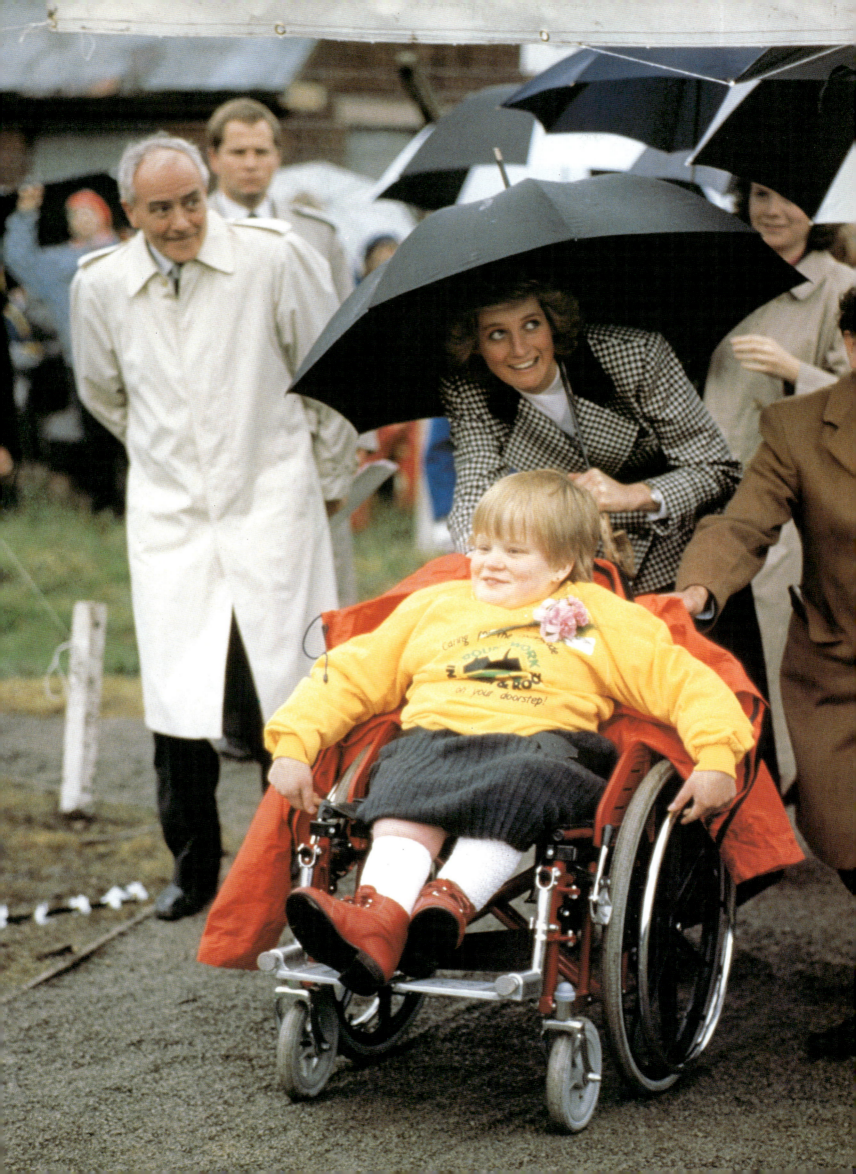

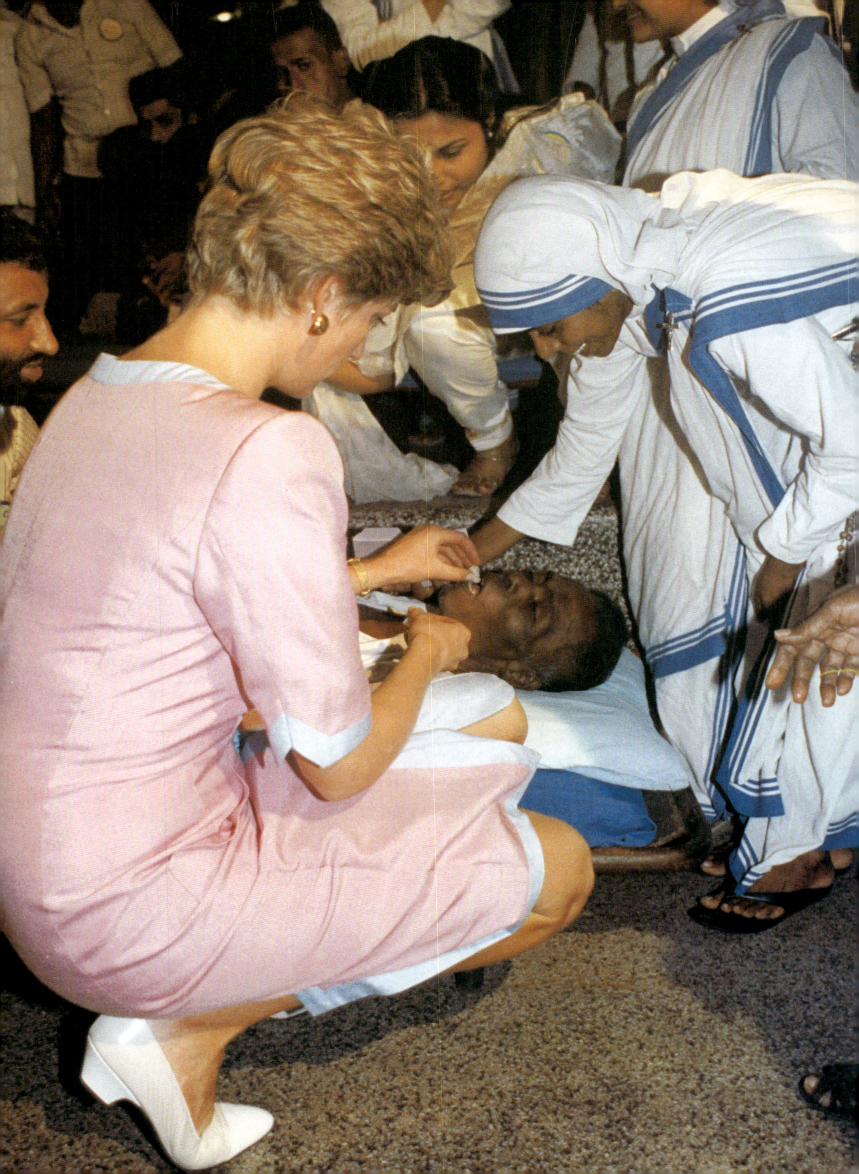

LEFT: *The twentieth-century equivalent of the medieval belief that a king's touch could cure? Princess Diana feeding a dying man during a visit to Mother Theresa's Hospice for the Dying, Calcutta, in February 1992.*

RIGHT: *Some of Diana's most important charity work was concerned with AIDS. Here she is opening an AIDS ward at the Middlesex Hospital, London.*

BELOW: *When the Waleses went on a five-day official tour of Brazil in April 1991, Diana insisted on including a visit to AIDS patients at the university hospital, Rio de Janeiro.*

LEFT: *Charity galas were an essential and pleasurable feature of the Princess's fundraising work; here (pregnant with William) she is seen meeting screen goddess Elizabeth Taylor after the gala premier of* Little Foxes *in which Taylor starred.*

RIGHT: *Diana with New Zealand soprano Dame Kiri te Kanawa at a concert in aid of Westminster Children's Hospital.*

BELOW: *Meeting Dynasty star Joan Collins and fashion designer and former Barnado's boy Bruce Oldfield at a charity dinner in aid of Dr Barnado's Children's Homes; the eye-catching gold dress is an Oldfield design.*

PREVIOUS PAGES: *Surrounded by New York's Finest, Diana met an enthusiastic crowd outside Harlem Hospital, where she visited the paediatric AIDS clinic in February 1989.*

ABOVE: *During a visit to Washington DC in 1990 the Princess received a t-shirt and hat on which were written 'Spread the word not the virus' as she left Grandpa's House, a centre for abandoned and abused children.*

RIGHT: *Diana shaking hands with a leper child at Sitanala leprosy hospital during a visit to Indonesia with Prince Charles in 1989. The gesture was a significant one in · helping to dispel the continuing myths about the disease.*

FAR RIGHT: *Receiving a bouquet of flowers at a HelpAge home in Brussels during a visit to open the new Brussels office of Help the Aged International in 1990.*

TOP: *At the Peto Institute, Budapest, in May 1990 Diana chats with Dawn Rogers, who has learned to walk as a result of specialist care.*

ABOVE: *Playing the piano for Czechoslovak orphans at Prague Castle during an official tour, May 1991.*

RIGHT: *At ease with a five-year-old leukaemia patient at the Ontario Regional Cancer Centre in October 1991.*

CHAPTER 6

A WORKING PRINCESS: STATE AND FORMAL OCCASIONS

RIGHT: *For her first State Opening of Parliament on 4 November 1989, the Princess was the focus of all eyes in her white chiffon dress, tiara and four-strand pearl choker on loan from the Queen. 'She absolutely lit up the old place,' said one appreciative MP, but perhaps her husband was less impressed with this subconscious scene-stealing.*

RIGHT: *Photographed with a Gurkha regiment in the Khyber Pass during her first major solo trip to Pakistan, in 1991. This proved a significant turning point in Diana's evolution into an independent princess.*

The royal family work to a rigid timetable, planned out in meticulous detail months in advance, and the Princess of Wales was no exception to the rule. When she was in residence in the apartments she maintained at Kensington Palace, she drove herself to work each morning. The original plan was for Kensington Palace to house the Prince and Princess's office suites as well as their private rooms, and it was Diana who put her foot down at the idea of 'living over the shop'. So she drove herself to work in St James's Palace, pleasantly situated in the heart of London's West End between Green Park and St James's Park, a stone's throw from Buckingham Palace.

Many of Diana's staff were naval officers, who could be commanding frigates one moment and drafting royal speeches the next; they returned to sea after a two-year secondment. One royal observer described them, tellingly, as 'noted for their short haircuts, gleaming shoes, and the healthy pinkness of people who had early morning showers, All Bran, and a run in the park before reaching their desks each morning eager and freshly bright.' The seven ladies-in-waiting formed the backbone of the operation, with two or more always in attendance at engagements.

The pace heated up in the Princess's offices when she began to surround herself with a younger and more dynamic team than the standard middle-aged courtiers.

She was now one of the more hard-working of the royals in her own right; the Prince of Wales seemed deliberately to leave 'meet the people' engagements to his wife whilst he concentrated on discussions and working lunches with teams of experts.

The programme was planned at six-monthly intervals in June and December, with equerries, private secretaries, ladies-in-waiting and detectives all involved. Before an engagement was accepted a draft itinerary had to be provided; if approved, a detective and an equerry would go on a preliminary visit; and the final programme was sent to every department in St James's Palace.

Security was one of the most irksome aspects of royal life. Diana and her staff could never forget that in every crowd might lurk a potential assassin. The constant presence at her side of a bodyguard was an unwelcome reminder of the constraints of her position; even a casual lunch with a friend in a Knightsbridge restaurant was shadowed by a discreet form at a nearby table. An ambulance and a fire engine were on permanent standby.

The Princess's reaction to this ever-present threat was a characteristically practical one. At the SAS (Special Air Services) headquarters in Hereford she was put through a rigorous anti-terrorist driving course which included avoiding thunderflashes and smoke bombs. She was an extremely fast and competent driver, being flagged down more than once by speed police on her journeys between

Highgrove and London. She had also attended the Metropolitan Police weapons' training centre, where she was taught to use a .38 caliber Smith & Wesson revolver and machine pistol.

There are some obligatory fixed points in the royal calendar, known to insiders as 'MOBG' — morally obliged to go — that members of the royal family have to attend. These include the Trooping of the Colour, the Queen's official Birthday Parade on the second Saturday in June. A major review of the Queen's ceremonial troops on Horse Guards Parade in central London, this is one of the most spectacular displays of pageantry in the world. The Braemar Highland Games at the beginning of September is one of the few public occasions for which the Queen breaks her Balmoral summer holiday, and her guests are also expected to attend. November brings both the State Opening of Parliament, where monarchy meets democracy in another elegant and colourful ceremony, and the more sombre Remembrance Day parade.

It was the royal tours, however, which both attracted the most media attention and required the most detailed and arduous planning. The first major tour for the fledgling Princess was Australia in 1982, shortly after the birth of Prince William. It was staggeringly successful, but its very success made it a punishing endurance test. Out of a population of 17 million, around one million of those turned out to see the royal couple, and at times the welcome bordered on hysteria. No one in the royal party, let alone the inexperienced Diana, had met this kind of reception before and it was Diana the crowds wanted; when they got Prince Charles on their side of the streets during the numerous royal walkabouts, they complained bitterly. This was the first manifestation of the now famil-

iar phenomenon of Princess as Megastar; if seasoned courtiers were taken aback, the unfortunate Diana was devastated and would weep with nervous exhaustion at the end of yet another long, exposed day.

With experience, however, came confidence; she adapted with charm and efficiency to the peculiar rhythm of royal tours, described by one royal newshound as 'a combination of stultifying boredom, sublime settings, and ridiculous red tape.' Her sense of humour certainly helped her cope with the elaborate absurdities laid on by over-enthusiastic locals — like the bare earth painted green in Halifax, Nova Scotia, to match the specially laid turf. Sumptuousness reached its peak in the Gulf in 1986, when the Princess was given several gorgeous suites of jewellery, including a diamond choker nearly two inches wide from the Emir of Kuwait. In Saudi Arabia their hosts transferred the entire contents of a palace into the desert, Persian carpets and all, so that the royal couple could enjoy a typically Arab desert banquet. Amid all the glamour, however, the Princess never forgot that each visit had a purpose: the Gulf tour was to encourage investment in British expertise.

Other major royal tours included Washington in 1985; Canada in 1986 to open EXPO 86 in Vancouver; West Germany in 1987; Paris and the Far East in 1988; Nigeria, Italy and Japan in 1990; and India and the ill-fated Korean tour in 1992. 1991 saw a new departure, with the Princess on her first major solo trip, to Pakistan, and in March 1992 she instituted another innovation, taking her sister Sarah to Budapest in the role of lady-in-waiting.

After her divorce from Prince Charles, Diana's tours and visits continued. Indeed, those to Angola and Bosnia raised the issue of landmines to the international stage.

LEFT: *Dressed for the heat in Luxor, Egypt, spring 1992.*

ABOVE: *Dressed for the cold with President Vaclav Havel of Czechoslovakia at a war cemetery in Prague, spring 1991.*

ABOVE AND ABOVE RIGHT: *Two very different forms of entertainment on the Gulf tour, 1986: a desert banquet and a formal feast.*

RIGHT: *Rubbing noses is a traditional Maori greeting: New Zealand, 1988.*

FAR RIGHT: *A typically romantic Spanish gesture welcomes the Princess on a formal visit to Madrid.*

CHAPTER 7

GOODBYE ENGLAND'S ROSE

ABOVE: *Diana alone — in front of the Taj Mahal in February 1992.*

RIGHT: *The Princess with the pyramids as a backdrop; Giza, Egypt, March 1992.*

'The end of a fairytale' was how the headlines summed up the announcement by Buckingham Palace on 9 December 1992 that Prince Charles and Princess Diana were to separate. The official statement asserted: 'Their Royal Highnesses have no plans to divorce and their constitutional positions are unaffected. Their decision has been reached amicably, and they will both continue to participate fully in the upbringing of their children . . .'

It was obvious, however, that the Prince and Princess's separation had been anything but amicable and that Diana's constitutional position would be wholly altered. The world's favourite princess could never become Queen.

Yet it was to be almost four long years before the marriage was formally ended by a divorce. They were not the happiest years for Diana but she managed to use them constructively to rebuild a life alone. She had rediscovered something of the girl-about-town lifestyle which she had relished all too briefly before her engagement. She also strove to establish herself as a serious international stateswoman — in her own words, an 'ambassador for Britain' and a 'queen of people's hearts'. She undertook many successful tours and espoused the cause of many charities, sometimes publicly but as often doing her good works in private and without publicity. Unannounced, she made late-night hospital visits to the bedsides of the terminally ill and even took her sons with her on a trip to a hostel for the homeless.

The press spotlight never left her, however, and sometimes became too much for her to bear. On 3 December 1993, as a guest at a London charity lunch, she tearfully announced that 'overwhelming media attention' had been so 'hard to bear' that she was bowing out of most of her public duties in favour of private charitable work and the job of raising her sons William and Harry.

Diana felt a deep sense of abandonment in those difficult early years of separation from Charles — and responded by throwing herself into work, from secretly visiting London hospitals at dead of night to very publicly accepting a 'Humanitarian of the Year' award in New York from Henry Kissinger. But she received little practical help from Buckingham Palace officials and scant support from the Royal Family. She reacted by snubbing occasions like the Queen's traditional Christmas lunches at Sandringham and instead spent them alone at Kensington Palace.

The long-awaited announcement that the Prince and Princess of Wales would finally divorce came on 28 February 1996, although months of deadlock followed before terms were agreed. When the 15-year marriage was officially ended on 28 August 1996, the British public were pleased to learn that Diana had received a £17 million (c$25½ million) settlement — but were shocked to discover that she was to suffer the humiliation of being stripped of the title 'Her Royal Highness'.

Sympathy and love flowed out to the people's favourite royal, now to be titled simply 'Diana, Princess of Wales'. She seemed to take comfort from this groundswell of public support and, although she had relinquished patronage of one hundred of her charities, she threw herself into high-profile support of those that she still actively supported. Principal among Diana's causes were the Red Cross, the National AIDS Trust, the Centrepoint charity for the homeless, the Leprosy Mission and two of Britain's premier children's hospitals, the Royal Marsden and Great Ormond Street.

The birth of the new 'go it alone' Diana was signalled by the £2 million ($3 million) American charity auction of her designer dresses in June 1997 (solely the idea of her elder son). That was the glamorous side of her work. Less so but far more influential was her crusade to rid the world of landmines. Pictures of the compassionate princess stalking through the danger zones of Angola and hugging limbless victims were images that could never be forgotten — and never ignored by politicians who for decades had kept the issue off the diplomatic agenda.

Her own favourite photograph, however, was one in which she cradled a young cancer victim in Lahore, Pakistan. It showed her doing what she did best; reaching out to people and ignoring the established royal protocol of 'look but don't touch'. The Princess no longer cared about upsetting the Establishment. Her only wish was to bring comfort

to any who needed it. She was, nevertheless, deeply wounded when critics accused her of being a 'loose cannon' interfering in political issues.

Against this backdrop, Diana found her new role gruelling and deeply draining, but for the first time in her life she felt she was fully utilising her gift to communicate with and enrich the lives of ordinary people worldwide. It was only in her personal life that she seemed unfulfilled. Yet in the last days of her life, Diana found the happiness that had eluded her for so long.

On 2 August 1997 Diana was photographed aboard a yacht off Sardinia sharing a tender kiss with Dodi Fayed, the film producer son of Mohammed Al Fayed, owner of the top people's store Harrods. They spent blissful days together in the South of France and Dodi's London apartment, interrupted by a three-day mission by Diana to Bosnia in her campaign to eradicate landmines. There she wept as she talked to children injured or bereaved by these leftover weapons of war. She comforted a sobbing mother mourning her dead son in Tuzla cemetery. Then she returned to Dodi's arms. She made no attempt to hide her love for him. She had, it seemed, found the true soulmate she had sought for so long.

On the night of Saturday, 30 August, Diana and Dodi dined at the Fayed-owned Ritz hotel in Paris before stepping into the back of a limousine to be driven the mile to Dodi's French home. On the brief journey, pursued by paparazzi photographers on motorbikes, the Mercedes swept at speed into an underpass at the Place de l'Alma beside the River Seine and crashed, killing the driver and Dodi Fayed.

ABOVE: *Diana in Angola wearing flak jacket and head visor.*

BELOW RIGHT: *A beautiful and radiant Diana in May 1997.*

After cutting her from the wreckage of the car, doctors embarked on a three-hour battle to save Diana's life. But at about four o'clock on the morning of 31 August 1997, they were forced to admit defeat. The world's most famous lady was dead.

Diana's body was flown back to Britain and the nation embarked on an unprecedented and unashamed public display of mourning. On Saturday, 6 September, Diana's coffin, draped in a flag bearing the Royal Family's coat of arms, left Kensington Palace on a gun carriage drawn by six horses. The Princes William and Harry — brave beyond their 15 and 12 years — walked behind it, past weeping crowds of one million Britons who thronged the route. Flanking the Princes were their father Prince Charles, their grandfather Prince Philip and their uncle, Diana's younger brother Charles Earl Spencer, as the cortege made its slow journey through Hyde Park and alongside Buckingham Palace to Westminster Abbey.

There, in a moving hour-long funeral service, the Queen and the rest of the Royal Family, a host of statesmen and celebrities, 30 million Britons and 2.5 billion others who watched on television worldwide saw tributes — and tears aplenty — flow. Then the Princess's body was driven to Althorp, Northamptonshire, for a private burial on a tiny island in a lake on the Spencer family estate.

Diana was home.

IN WESTMINSTER ABBEY DIANA'S FRIEND, SINGER ELTON JOHN, MOVINGLY PUT INTO WORDS AND MUSIC THE THOUGHTS OF A GRIEVING WORLD THAT HAD BEEN TOUCHED BY THE SHORT 36-YEAR LIFE OF DIANA PRINCESS OF WALES . . .

Goodbye England's Rose;
May you ever grow in our hearts.
You were the grace that placed itself
Where lives were torn apart.
You called out to our country
And you whispered to those in pain.
Now you belong to heaven,
And the stars spell out your name.

And it seems to me you lived your life
Like a candle in the wind:
Never fading with the sunset
When the rain set in.
And your footsteps will always fall here,
along England's greenest hills.
Your candle's burned out long before
Your legend ever will.

Loveliness we've lost;
These empty days without your smile.
This torch we'll always carry
For our nation's golden child.
And even though we try,
The truth brings us to tears;
All our words cannot express
The joy you brought us through the years.

And it seems to me you lived your life
Like a candle in the wind:
Never fading with the sunset
When the rain set in.
And your footsteps will always fall here,
along England's greenest hills.
Your candle's burned out long before
Your legend ever will.

Goodbye England's rose:
May you ever grow in our hearts.
You were the grace that placed itself
Where lives were torn apart.
Goodbye England's rose,
From a country lost without your soul,
Who'll miss the wings of your compassion
More than you'll ever know.

And it seems to me you lived your life
Like a candle in the wind:
Never fading with the sunset
When the rain set in.
And your footsteps will always fall here,
along England's greenest hills.
Your candle's burned out long before
Your legend ever will.

93

ABOVE: *One enduring legacy Diana left behind was a future heir to the throne. Prince William, the boy born to be king, had the eyes of the world focused on him and his younger brother Harry at the funeral. They acquitted themselves magnificently, despite their tender ages of 15 and 12. Here, the Princes — William left and Harry — bow their heads as their mother's coffin is taken out of Westminster Abbey following the funeral service.*

LEFT: *The most poignant photograph of all — a wreath with the message 'Mummy' on top of the Princess's coffin as it leaves Westminster Abbey.*

ABOVE RIGHT: *Earl Spencer addresses the congregation in front of his sister's coffin.*

I stand before you today the representative of a family in grief, in a country in mourning, before a world in shock.

We are all united not only in our desire to pay our respects to Diana but rather in our need to do so.

For such was her extraordinary appeal that the tens of millions of people taking part in this service all over the world via television and radio who never actually met her, feel that they too lost someone close to them in the early hours of Sunday morning. It is a more remarkable tribute to Diana than I can ever hope to offer her today.

Diana was the very essence of compassion, of duty, of style, of beauty. All over the world she was a symbol of selfless humanity. All over the world, a standard bearer for the rights of the truly downtrodden, a very British girl who transcended nationality. Someone with a natural nobility who was classless and who proved in the last years that she needed no royal title to continue her particular brand of magic.

Today is our chance to say thank you for the way you brightened our lives, even though God granted you but half a life. We will all feel cheated always that you were taken from us so young and yet we must learn to be grateful that you came along at all. Only now that you are gone do we truly appreciate what we are now without and we want you to know that life without you is very, very difficult.

We have all despaired at our loss over the past week and only the strength of the message you gave us through your years of giving has afforded us the strength to move forward.

There is a temptation to canonise your memory, there is no need to do so. You stand tall enough as a human being of unique qualities not to need to be seen as a saint. Indeed to sanctify your memory would be to miss out on the very core of your being, your wonderfully mischievous sense of humour with a laugh that bent you double.

Your joy for life transmitted where ever you took your smile and the sparkle in those unforgettable eyes. Your boundless energy which you could barely contain.

But your greatest gift was your intuition and it was a gift you used wisely. This is what underpinned all your other wonderful attributes and if we look to analyse what it was about you that had such a wide appeal we find it in your instinctive feel for what was really important in all our lives. Without your God-given sensitivity we would be immersed in greater ignorance at the anguish of Aids and HIV sufferers, the plight of the homeless, the isolation of lepers, the random destruction of landmines.

Diana explained to me once that it was her innermost feelings of suffering that made it possible to connect with her constituency of the rejected. And here we come to another truth about her. For all the status, the glamour, the applause, Diana remained throughout a very insecure person at heart, almost childlike in her desire to do good for others so she could release herself from deep feelings of unworthiness of which her eating disorders were merely a symptom.

95

The world sensed this part of her character and cherished her for her vulnerability while admiring her for her honesty.

The last time I saw Diana was on July 1, her birthday in London, when typically she was not taking time to celebrate her special day with friends but was guest of honour at a special charity fundraising evening. She sparkled of course, but I would rather cherish the days I spent with her in March when she came to visit me and my children in our home in South Africa. I am proud of the fact, apart from when she was on display meeting President Mandela, we managed to stop the ever-present paparazzi from getting a single picture of her — that meant a lot to her.

These were days I will always treasure. It was if we had been transported back to our childhood when we spent such an enormous amount of time together — the two youngest in the family.

Fundamentally she had not changed at all from the big sister who mothered me as a baby, fought with me at school and endured those long train journeys between our parents' homes with me at weekends.

It is a tribute to her levelheadedness and strength that despite the most bizarré-like life imaginable after her childhood, she remained intact, true to herself.

There is no doubt that she was looking for a new direction in her life at this time. She talked endlessly of getting away from England, mainly because of the treatment that she received at the hands of the newspapers. I don't think she ever understood why her genuinely good intentions were sneered at by the media, why there appeared to be a permanent quest on their behalf to bring her down. It is baffling.

My own and only explanation is that genuine goodness is threatening to those at the opposite end of the moral spectrum. It is a point to remember that of all the ironies about Diana, perhaps the greatest was this — a girl given the name of the ancient goddess of hunting was, in the end, the most hunted person of the modern age.

She would want us today to pledge ourselves to protecting her beloved boys William and Harry from a similar fate and I do this here Diana on your behalf. We will not allow them to suffer the anguish that used regularly to drive you to tearful despair.

And beyond that, on behalf of your mother and sisters, I pledge that we, your blood family, will do all we can to continue the imaginative way in which you were steering these two exceptional young men so that their souls are not simply immersed by duty and tradition but can sing openly as you planned.

We fully respect the heritage into which they have both been born and will always respect and encourage them in their royal role but we, like you, recognise the need for them to experience as many different aspects of life as possible to arm them spiritually and emotionally for the years ahead. I know you would have expected nothing less from us.

William and Harry, we all care desperately for you today. We are all chewed up with the sadness at the loss of a woman who was not even our mother. How great your suffering is, we cannot imagine.

I would like to end by thanking God for the small mercies he has shown us at this dreadful time. For taking Diana at her most beautiful and radiant and when she had joy in her private life. Above all we give thanks for the life of a woman I am so proud to be able to call my sister, the unique, the complex, the extraordinary and irreplaceable Diana, whose beauty, both internal and external, will never be extinguished from our minds.

ABOVE LEFT: *At a visit to Northwick Park Hospital, July 1997.*

BELOW: *'The Oval' a tiny island in a lake on the Spencer family estate at Althorp, where the Princess was laid to rest.*